# John F. Kennedy

MIKE WILSON

GW00703274

ALBSU
Registered Charity No. 1003969
The Basic Skills Unit

In May 1962,
Marilyn Monroe went to a birthday party.
The President of the United States,
John Fitzgerald Kennedy,
was 45 years old.

Marilyn blew kisses at Kennedy,
and sang "Happy Birthday".

Some people began to think
Marilyn and JFK were having an affair.

Three months later, Marilyn was dead.
Some say she was murdered,
because she knew too much.

Next year, President Kennedy was dead too,
shot in the head in Dallas, Texas.

Both of these deaths
were surrounded by gossip and mystery.
We may never know all the facts
about the life and death
of John F Kennedy.

# Young Jack

John F Kennedy was born in Boston,
in 1917.
He was one of 9 children
in an Irish Catholic family.

The Kennedys were rich.
His father, Joseph,
was US Ambassador to Britain
before World War II.

The family were very close,
but Joseph pushed his sons hard.
He wanted one of them
to be the first Catholic
to become President of the United States.

John (who was also known as Jack)
fought in World War II on a gun-boat.

He won a medal for bravery,
and in 1946,
he went into politics with the Democrats
as a war-hero.

He won the election for President in 1960,
but he only won by a few votes.
The other candidate was the Republican,
Richard Nixon.

# The President

The new President was 43,
the youngest US President ever.

In a few months
he made his first big mistake.

On April 17th 1961
15,000 Cuban exiles
landed in the Bay of Pigs in Cuba.

They had US guns
and were helped by the CIA.
They wanted to bring down Fidel Castro,
the Communist leader in Cuba.

The raid was a flop,
and President Kennedy had to back down.
He sent food and medicine to Cuba
to say sorry.

But the CIA still went on
with secret plans to kill Castro.

Next year, in October 1962,
US planes spotted nuclear missiles
– built by Russia –
right on their doorstep in Cuba.

President Kennedy told the Russians
to remove the rockets.
If they didn't, America would bomb them,
and start a nuclear war.

For 13 days,
the world held its breath.

Then the Russians backed down.
The Cuban Crisis was over.

Kennedy had won
the deadly game of bluff.

After the Cuban Crisis,
President Kennedy had plans
to be more friendly with Russia.

He had plans
to get America out of Vietnam.
And he wanted to give more rights
to black people and poor people
all over America.

But all his plans were cut short
on November 22nd, 1963,
in Dallas, Texas.

# Dallas

Kennedy went to Texas
because he had political enemies there,
and he wanted to win them to his side.

At noon a line of cars left the airport
and drove JFK into town.
The President sat in an open car,
waving to the crowds.

In the car with him
were his wife, Jackie Kennedy
and the Governor of Texas,
John Connally and his wife.
There were no security men
in the car to protect the President.

The car slowed as it turned out of Elm Street.

For the next 6 seconds,
the air was full of rifle fire.

The President fell back,
covering his wife with blood.
He had been hit in the neck, the back,
and in the side of the head.

The shooting seemed to come
from two places at the same time:
from a building
a long way behind the President's car;
and from some trees just in front.

The President's car raced to hospital,
but JFK could not be saved.

A few hours later,
police arrested Lee Harvey Oswald
for the murder of John F Kennedy.

Oswald was a poor, strange no-hoper.
He was mixed up in crime
and left wing politics.
He was known to the FBI and the CIA.

He was in Dallas on the day of the murder.
He worked in the building
the rifle shots came from.
But he was a poor shot,
and he could not have fired all the bullets
which hit the President and 2 other men.


Did Oswald really shoot Kennedy?
Did he work alone or did he have help?
Or was he innocent?
Was he "set up" by other people?

We will never know Oswald's story.
Two days after his arrest,
he was shot and killed by Jack Ruby,
who worked for the FBI and the CIA.

Jack Ruby died in prison a few years later.

# That Was The President . . .

President John F Kennedy
was still young and handsome
when he died.

He was the best-loved President in America
since Abraham Lincoln
(and Lincoln was also shot and killed, in 1865).

We may never find out
how John F Kennedy was murdered,
or why he had to die.

Now, over 30 years on,
America remembers the President as a hero.

They see his death
as the death of Hope.

They see his murder
as the murder of the American Dream.